GROWING IN THE GOSPEL

EXAMINING THE BOOK OF THE REVELATION BY SYMBOLISM

With a taste of how it can affect the Church today - UPDATED

Michael Harvey Koplitz

Table of Contents

Introduction

The Book of Revelation is the most challenging book in the New Testament to read. It contains over one thousand symbols, of which many come from the Old Testament. Before attempting to digest this book, the reader should be familiar with Daniel, Ezekiel, and Isaiah's books. Knowing the minor prophets will help in the study.

Revelation deals with future events. The book's events have been interpreted over the past two thousand years to be what was happening. Since the book claims to tell its reader about the end of time, until the end comes, it is impossible to equate the book's events to present times.

The book is based on a Hebraic apocalyptic liturgy. The central theme is that things are bad; things will get worse. Eventually, the LORD will step in and remake Heaven and Earth for the righteous people. This theme of Hebraic apocalyptic books is the theme of Revelation. There are many interpretations of the book that you may and may not find. Trying to discover the truth of this book will be difficult because of the many interpretations.

A valuable tool for the understanding of Revelation is to examine each of the symbols. This book is not a book that can be read literally. Every passage is filled with metaphors, similes, and symbolism. The reader is encouraged to place all of what they heard in the Church about Revelation off to the side before beginning. Try not to have a conceived notion of what will be found. That will allow the words of the book to speak.

Reading the Revelation and understanding it is a considerable challenge. If you have an open mind and are ready to see the book for what it is, then let us begin the journey.

An Outline of the Revelation

1. Rev 1:1-8, John Introduces the book

2. Rev 1:9-20, The Great Voice, the Vision of the Son of Man Who Commissions John to write.

3. Rev 2:1-3:22 – John Writes to the Angels

   - 2:1-7, Ephesus

   - 2:8-11, Smyrna

   - 2:12-17, Pergamum

   - 2:18-29, Thyatira

   - 3:1-6, Sardis

   - 3:7-13, Philadelphia

   - 3:14-22, Laodicea

4. Rev 4:1-11, vision of God's Throne in Heaven

5. Rev 5:1-14, vision of the Divine Scroll and the Lamb

6. Rev 6:1-17, John sees the seals opened

7. Rev 7:1-17, concerning those seals, and a vision of the Great multitude

   - 7:1-8, the 144,000 of Israel are sealed

   - 7:9-17, the multitude of every nation

8. Rev 8:1-9:21, the seventh seal and the seven angels with seven trumpets

9. Rev 10:1-11, the vision of the strong angel and the command to prophesy

10. Rev 11:1-19, the two witnesses

11. Rev 12:1-18, Signs in Heaven: The woman and the dragon

12. Rev 13:1-18, the vision of two beasts

13. Rev 14:1-20, the lamb, the 144,000, the Eternal Gospel, and the human figure

    - 14:1-5, the song of the 144,000

    - 14:6-13, the message of the three angels

    - 14:14-20, the harvest of the Earth

14.   Rev 15:1-8, Another sign from heaven: The Sea of Glass and the song of those who conquered

15.   Rev 16:1-21, Seven angels and seven trumpets

16.   Rev 17:1-18, the vision of Babylon

17.   Rev 18:1-19:10, the Fall of Babylon

18.   Rev 19:11-21, Heavens Opens and the Riders on the White Horse appears

19.   Rev 20:1-15, Millennium and judgment

20.   Rev 21:1-22:5, the New Heaven, the New Earth, the New Jerusalem

21.   Rev 22:6-21, concluding saying

Revelation 2:1-7 – The Letter to the Angel at Ephesus

Ephesus was an important center of Christian life for the apostle Paul. The Bishop Ignatius of Antioch saw Ephesus as the center of Christianity in the Asia Minor area (Ignatius claimed he was the child that Jesus referred to in the Gospels – when Jesus told them to be like "this child"). [1]

The seven-golden lamp stands in chapter 1, verse 13, represent the seven churches that are addressed by the letters. The seven stars are the seven angels of the churches. At the start of chapter two, we are told that Christ is walking among the seven stars and seventeen lamp stands. This is a reference to the book of Genesis when God walked near Adam and Eve after they had committed their sin (Genesis 3:8). This reference gives us an early sign that something is not correct with the seven churches.

Christ starts by congratulating the angel on his deeds, hard work and perseverance that has been happening at the church. Christ takes on a dual role. He is the comforter and the judge. By starting out with some words of congratulations Christ comforts the church at Ephesus for their success in ministry. However, since Christ is walking amongst them like God in the Garden, there is some judgment that is to follow.

They are commended for their "patient endurance." This is a characteristic of authentic Christian existence (refer to Luke 8:15; 21:19, Romans 5:3; 8:25, 1 Thessalonians 1:3). Endurance is persistence in faith when faced with the persecutions of the culture.[2] The church had endured evil people and a test from true and false prophets.

---

[1] L. Edited by Keck, The New Interpreters Bible Commentary, Volume XII vols. (Nashville, TN: Abingdon Press, 1998), page 574
[2] IBID, page 575

The opening compliment is then followed by a critical evaluation of the current situation. The indictment is that the church has lost its first love. This is a reference to Matthew 24:12 which tells us that because of an increase in wickedness, the love of most will grow cold, but he who stands firm to the end will be saved. It is possible that through the false prophets and different heretical movements of that day, the church has forgotten its original mission and love for Christ.

The Montanist movement was strong in Asia Minor. This group of heretical Christians considered the God and Father of our Lord Jesus Christ to be a different God than the God of the Hebrew Scriptures. This group discounted the Hebrew Scriptures, especially the prophets, as not a part of Christianity. Perhaps the warning from Christ is to tell the church at Ephesus that they need to follow the correct values of Christianity.

w

Apparently, the movement inside the church toward false prophets must have been great. In verse 5 the church is told to repent. If they do not repent, then the lampstand, that is the church, will be removed from them. The church may have also let too much of the surrounding culture infiltrate it. The sinful nature of Roman culture would have entered the church through the conversion of the pagan gentiles. If the church became complacent to the will of the converts who wanted to keep their old pagan ways, then the church would not be a church of God but a pagan institution. If this happened, then certainly Christ would take the lamp stand away from them.

In repenting, the Scripture calls for the church to stop its sinful ways. It is important in repentance to recognize the sin, the error, the mistake, but it is also vitally important that the practice be stopped. The letter to Ephesus does not explain in any detail what these sins were. Paul's letter to the church at Ephesus can give some sign of the situation. The pressures from outside of the church that existed in Paul's time did still exist by the end of the first century

CE. Sometimes, these pressures were amplified when, after 70 CE Christianity broke away from its Jewish heritage.

A message from this letter is that the church must not allow the culture that it lives in to dictate what is right or wrong. The first deciding factor on right or wrong must be God's word, the Scripture. To use any other measuring tool is opposing God. Throughout Christ's ministry, we can see that He was counter cultural. The culture of Christ's day was corrupt when measured against the Law of God. The culture did not change that much seventy years later. The same problems and pressures existed.

God tells us today not to let the same thing happen. Sufficient theologians believe that the church today in the United States is in the same circumstances as the church was in the first century. Politicians and civic groups have been working desperately to exclude the church from society. Churches have been accepting anti-biblical behaviors and attitudes and justifying them as acceptable, which truly opposes God's word.

If the churches continue to accept the culture's influence on them, that is what the Bible says is wrong, then the prophecy for Ephesus will come true for today's church.

Revelation 2:8-11 – The Church at Smyrna

This letter to the Church at Smyrna comes from the one who is the first and the last, the resurrected one, Jesus the Christ. This church was undergoing an affliction. The Greek word used here is "thlipsis" which is used to show a time of crisis and catastrophe that marks the climax of history.[3] Is the church being told that they are suffering in the end times? If so, then their end times would have to be defined differently than the end times of the world. The end times here could refer to the end of the church at Smyrna.

Satan is introduced into the Revelation for the first time through the letter to Smyrna. Those who overcome Satan will become a part of the heavenly realm. It is interesting that even though Christ has defeated Satan, Satan can still influence the church's people. Some activities of Satan are described by the church. Some people will be put into prison because of their faith, while others will face death. These verses tell us that some people of Smyrna will die for their faith in God.

The sense of Satan's persecution of the church has an overtone of the battle between God and Satan in the book of Job. Job stayed faithful to God no matter what Satan did to him. The people at Smyrna were being told the same thing. Faced with adversity, the people must remain loyal to Christ. If they were to die because of their opposition to Satan, God would reward them for their faithfulness.

Does the church follow the mission that Christ placed before it, even in the light of adversity? Do we rally together to "fix" the church, or do we sit back in apathy? Can we identify the true nature of the problem? Unfortunately, people have such differing views and opinions, combined with the difficulty of letting the Spirit shine through that it is difficult to hear God's voice.

---

[3] L. Edited by Keck, <u>The New Interpreters Bible Commentary</u>, Volume XII vols. (Nashville, TN: Abingdon Press, 1998), page 576

God is not saying in this letter that the church at Smyrna would survive. Instead, he is saying that those in the church who work for God will be saved. Those who stand up to adversity and continue to have faith in God will be admitted into heaven.

Revelation 2:18-29

The letter to the angel at Thyatira is the longest of the seven letters sent to the seven angels of the seven churches. It is also the only reference to the Son of God made in the book of Revelation.[4] Part of the compliments from the Son of God is that the situation has improved for the church at Thyatira. This commendation is followed by solid criticism.

The criticism starts regarding the toleration of Jezebel. Jezebel was the wife of King Ahab (2 Kings 9). 2 Kings 9:22 hints that she had some prophetic powers.[5] Jezebel was a strong opponent of the true prophet of the Lord who was Elijah. He was a zealous opponent of the idolatrous compromises that had occurred under the reign of King Ahab, which integrated Baal worship with God worship. Baal worship led Israel away from their true God.

The 'fornication' referred to in verse 20 is probably best understood metaphorically as the compromises between the practices of the church and the culture that resulted in idolatry and compromised the distinctiveness of life of the Christian church, which is a central feature of Revelation.[6] Since the Church developed as an offshoot of Judaism, the Church would have collected on the tradition of Judaism that the church had to stand out in its practices from the rest of the world. This was done by God so that His people would stand out from the rest of the people of the world. The laws and regulations found in Leviticus and Numbers caused God's chosen people to be different and sanctified for God. Jesus stood out as different even inside the Jewish culture of His day. This concept of being different, therefore being godly (sanctified), doing God's work and living God's life rather than by the ways of the culture, would cause the Christian Church to stand apart. This was not occurring in Thyatira. Members of the church were still practicing their pagan ways and conforming to the immorality of the culture. This problem seems to be prevalent in more than one of the seven churches.

---

[4] L. Edited by Keck, <u>The New Interpreters Bible Commentary</u>, Volume XII vols. (Nashville, TN: Abingdon Press, 1998), page 581

[5] IBID.

[6] IBID.

The letter shows this situation does not typify the entire church. The warning is to those who have not moved into conformity with the culture of the church to stay the course and that the reward will be an eternity in heaven. To this church, God tells them that just staying Christian and modeling Christ is more than enough of a burden for them.

Revelation 3:1-6 – The Letter to Sardis

In the first verse, we are told that Christ is the one holding the seven stars. The commendation of the church is not offered. Only one problem is voiced. What does it mean to be alive but dead? The answer is found in verse two. "I have not found your deeds complete in the sight of my God" (Rev 3:2). So, the church is doing something that is not contributing to the Kingdom of God. When the church has activities that do not prompt the Gospel of Christ, said activities are not deeds that God sees as pleasing in His sight. Everything that the church does must glorify God's name.

For example, when the church holds a potpie supper or summer picnic and does not use this opportunity to evangelize, then the activity is not one that God would support. Especially when these dinners raise funds because the church is not subsidizing the vital ministries of the Kingdom of God through them. It is not wrong to hold fundraising events that raise money for a mission project or a new ministry but to hold one because the congregation does not tithe is not biblical. Our special fundraisers should be held for missionary or evangelistic projects for the community.

Christ is pictured as a prosecuting counsel who has opened His book and has read the church's deeds.[7] The letter urges Sardis to repent for its sins and obey the Word of God. The reference to the "thief in the night" is first seen in Paul's letter to the Thessalonians (refer to Thessalonians 5:2). Christ will come when we least expect Him, and judgment will occur.

Verse four is a complement to the church. In this letter, the order of complement criticism is reversed. The reference to unsoiled clothing refers to those in the church who have remained faithful to Christ. They walk in white robes for they are worthy. White is the color of purity in Revelation.

---

[7] L. Keck, <u>The New Interpreter's Bible Commentary</u>, XII vols. (Nashville, TN: Abingdon Press, 1994). Page 583

Verse five tells us that Christ is a heavenly scribe with the right to erase names from the book of life. To be included in the book of life means that one's robes were made white by the blood of the Lamb and by obeying God. Christ is an accuser and not a judge. According to John's Gospel, Christ came not to judge the world. Here the addition of the prosecutor is added.[8]

This letter tells us that Christ could be our prosecutor on Judgment Day. How can this be? Is this not in direct conflict with the belief that Christ will be at our side on Judgment Day? Do we receive Christ's righteousness as believers (we say this during the Great Thanksgiving prayer at communion)? A fascinating theological representation of Christ is presented. To those who are washed in the blood, He saves. To those not washed in the blood, he will prosecute. Perhaps it fits the understanding of Christ. However, then where is grace in this letter?

---

[8] IBID.

Revelation 3:7-13 – Letter to Philadelphia

The "key of David" is used to reference Christ for the first time in Revelation. The construction of this formula can be found in Isaiah 22:22. Isaiah 22:22 is a reference to a promise to Eliakim, son of Hilkiah that he will succeed Shebna, the steward.[9] It is interesting to note how an Old Testament image is echoed in Revelation. It emphasizes that the author of Revelation had an excellent understanding of Isaiah. This reference to David reminds the readers that Christ is the Davidic messiah and that the Davidic covenant is still in force.

The holy one opens and closes a door in verses 7 and 8 is an image that will be used several times throughout the rest of the book.

The synagogue of Satan is brought up, which suggests a division inside the religious community. The division could be between those who call themselves Christians but still follow pagan ways and those who call themselves Christians and truly follow the ways of the Lamb. A promise made here by Christ is that the synagogue of Satan will be compelled to come to the angel and worship (echoing Isaiah 49:23 and 60:14).[10]

The commendation to the church is that it has been patient. The hour of trial is when Satan tries once more to win back all of humanity from God. The inference is that the battle between God and Satan has not ended with the resurrection of Christ. The author of Revelation does not accept the theology of the great battle between good and evil during the Easter vigil. It is again mentioned here that the war continues.

Christ is coming is an assurance to the people and not a threat, as it has been in the other letters. When Christ comes, God will place His name on the foreheads of those who are faithful. The apocalyptic reference to the new Jerusalem starts in this letter. Also, Christ will

---

[9] L. Keck, <u>The New Interpreter's Bible Commentary</u>, XII vols. (Nashville, TN: Abingdon Press, 1994). Page 384
[10] L. Keck, <u>The New Interpreter's Bible Commentary</u>. Page 385

receive a new name when he returns. Before the Babylonians invaded and destroyed Jerusalem, God sent an angel to place a mark on the forehead of the righteous. Therefore, this is an echo from the book of Ezekiel.

This last part has some attractive qualities. If Christ will receive a new name when He returns, how will we know if Jesus has returned? Certainly not by his name. Christ's return has been likened to a thief in the night because if His name is changed, we might not recognize Him (found in Paul's letters). Some believe that we live in the apocalypse because Christ has returned, and we did not notice it. That is why we must treat everyone we meet as if they were Christ.

8 - Revelation Chapter 4

Background information for this chapter:

1. Verse 2 – "In the Spirit" means that John is prophetically inspired in his vision.[11]
2. The number twenty-four is related to twenty-four books, Jewish writers assigned to the Hebrew canon, to the twelve tribes and twelve apostles, and the twenty-four orders of the priesthood. [12]
3. Greek accounts sometimes portrayed deities as appearing in white. White had been referred to as the color of good and black as the color of evil by some rabbis.[13]
4. The contrast between day and night, the latter being more associated with witchcraft and other demons.[14]
5. The sea of glass alludes to the sea in Solomon's Temple (1 Kings 7:23).[15]

This chapter of the book of Revelation is the author's vision of what heaven, the throne of God, looks like. According to his description, the author may see and sense the reality of God's sovereignty.[16] However, this vision is not the first time that heaven has been shown to us. In the Hebrew Scriptures, the opening of heaven can be found in Isaiah 6, especially in Ezekiel 1. 1 Enoch, which did not become a part of the Canon, has a description of heaven. After all, Enoch was the first human to be taken into heaven.

The trumpet is introduced in this vision and will play a major role in signifying the eschatological moment of the end of time and judgment day.[17] The trumpet was used in the Hebrew Scriptures to signify a "Godly" event. For example, the army of Israel circled Jericho

---

[11] C. Keener, The IVP Bible Background Commentary, New Testament
Downers Grove, Illinois vols. (Intervarsity Press: 1993, 1993). Page 776
[12] Keener, The IVP Bible Background Commentary. Page 776
[13] IBID.
[14] Keener, The IVP Bible Background Commentary. Page 777
[15] IBID.
[16] L. Keck, The New Interpreter's Bible Commentary, XII vols. (Nashville, TN: Abingdon Press, 1994). Page 591
[17] IBID.

seven times, then the priests blew their trumpets, and Jericho's walls fell. A voice calls out for John to "come up here," which is the same command Moses received from God on Sinai when he received God's Law. "What must take place" is another phrase that comes from the Hebrew Scriptures (Daniel 2:29, 45).

"The throne of God will play an important role in Revelation, though heaven plays virtually no part in John's vision of the new Jerusalem."[18] The throne of God is the place where the trinity resides, Father, Son, and Spirit. The throne of God pours forth lightning and thunder, echoing what happened on Mt. Sinai in Exodus 19:16. In that passage, the lightning and thunder were followed by a loud trumpet blast.

"The indebtedness to the language of Ezekiel's vision in Ezekiel 1 and 10 (especially), to Isaiah 6, and to the great theophany at Sinai in Exodus 19 is everywhere apparent in Revelation 4."[19] So the vision of the throne of God is a combination of earlier visions. The difference in this vision is that John concentrates his description on the throne of God. He describes what was going on where Ezekiel focused upon what God said during the vision.

Twenty-four other thrones surrounded the throne of God. Each of these "lesser" thrones are occupied by an elder thus creating a divine court (this is echoed in 1 Kings 22:19 and Isa 6:1). The elders are engaged in worship to God that is in unending worship. It is not clear who the twenty-four elders are. Isaiah 24:23 and 1 Chronicles 24:4 try to give the elders a face. In contrast to the Roman world, the emperor Domitian had a court of twenty-four lictors who surrounded him.[20] Is this a coincidence or a planned vision from God that the Roman emperor court would have the same number as the Divine Court?

---

[18] L. Keck, <u>The New Interpreter's Bible Commentary</u>. Page 591

[19] IBID.

[20] M. Boring, commentary Series, <u>Interpretation - A Bible Commentary for Teaching and Preaching</u>, Revelation vols. (Louisville, KT: John Knox Press, 1989). Page 103

Noise and fire preceded the Lord's descent on Mt. Sinai to give the Law to Moses. This action will be seen later in the book when God descends to the Earth.[21] John offers one interpretation of what he is seeing regarding the seven lamps that are before the throne of God (they represent the seven or sevenfold Spirit[s] of God). This imagery is echoed in Zechariah chapter 4. There the lamps are described as the "eyes" of the Lord.

The creatures full of eyes are creatures of pure insight and truthfully, the description of the creatures echoes Ezekiel 1. A difference here is that in Ezekiel 1, the beast had four faces, while here, John sees four different creatures. The creatures are worshiping God in ceaseless praise, shouting the same (almost the same) hymn found in Isaiah 6:3. The Greek word *pastorate* is used in the hymn, signifying that the one they worship is the Almighty God who existed before and existed thereafter.

This chapter contains a lot of imagery that has its origins in the Hebrew Scriptures. A lesson from this chapter could be seen in the worship that the elders were doing. This is a reminder to us that our worship is for God and not for ourselves. Also, as Paul writes, worship must be unceasing. Worship and sermons during these past years have moved from being evangelical toward being therapeutic. The church needs to learn from this chapter that worship is not a time for a therapy session. It is a time to worship and glorify God.

Worship is directed to God. It is our sign of appreciation and gratitude. It is a time for the Spirit to speak to us about what we should and must be doing to satisfy the Lord. Evangelistic worship and preaching is the key to the church's success. We must model the worship found in chapter 4 of Revelation.

---

[21] L. Keck, <u>The New Interpreter's Bible Commentary</u>. Page 592

9 - Revelation Chapter 5

Chapter 5 continues where chapter 4 leaves off with John in his vision of the throne room of Heaven. He sees the right hand of God holding a scroll with writing on both sides of it and sealed with seven seals. This scroll causes John some pain. He wants to know what the scroll says. The sealed scroll echoes Jeremiah 32:9-10 and especially Isaiah 29:11. In these passages, especially Isaiah 29:11, the concern is expressed about a scroll with writings on it that cannot be opened.[22] Later in Revelation, we will learn what was written on the scroll.

John weeps because no one is worthy in Heaven, Earth, or even below Earth to open the scrolls. This adds to the belief that he was very concerned about the contents of the scroll. The beginning of the description of the end of time will start with the reading of the scroll. "John mourns the fact that the process of justice and judgment is being delayed."[23] This is an assumption that at this point in the vision, John is geared toward judgment. This thinking fits into the theme of apocalyptic literature. The view is that times are bad, times will worsen, God will intervene by sending Christ, the new Jerusalem and the new Heaven will be created, and judgment will come.

No one is worthy of opening the scrolls. No, that is not true. The slaughtered lamb of God can open the scroll. The lamb almost magically appears in the center of the throne room. Throughout the history of interpreting this book, it is assumed that the lamb is Jesus.

The description does not fit Jesus. The lamb has seven horns and seven eyes. This is not a typical description of the Savior.

---

[22] L. Keck, ed., "Vision of the Divine Scroll and the Lamb," *The New Interpreters Bible Commentary*, vol. 12, *Hebrews, James, Peter, John, Jude, Revelation*, Keck, L., 600-605 (Abingdon, Tenn: *Abingdon Press 1998*).

[23] Keck, "Vision of the Divine Scroll and the Lamb".

The lamb's blood was used in Egypt when the Children of Israel were told to place the blood on the doorways and lentils of their homes so that the angel of death could pass over their homes (Exodus 12:22-23).[24] The hymn found in verses 9 & 10 celebrates that the blood of the slaughtered lamb paid a ransom for God for all the people of the Earth. That fits the Jesus tradition, but the eyes and horns do not. Perhaps the image of the lamb is not of Jesus, but instead of the lamb that saved the people in Egypt. Eventually, the scroll will be opened, and the pronouncement made is not very good. Why would the Savior of the world pronounce a sentence of death in the world? The verses that follow describe the lamb as an image of Jesus. However, the lamb is not sitting on any throne. Jesus tells us in the Gospels that He will be seated at the right hand of God in heaven.

Four beasts surround the lamb, which is a remarkable parallel to Daniel 7:7, where Daniel saw the four beasts of heaven. In Daniel, the animals were symbolic of the mighty kings of the Earth, while in Revelation, they have a different role that has not yet been revealed to us.[25] The lamb takes the scroll from God without permission. The lamb did not request the scroll or request it. The elders fall and worship the lamb in the same way that they worship God. Of course, this leads us back to the idea that the lamb is Christ.

Perhaps a theme out of this chapter of Revelation is that each of us must determine who or what our savior is. For many people, Jesus is not their Savior. Our culture permits forms of idolatry to become one's savior. For example, money, wealth, power, control are all motivators that draw people away from God and to these false "saviors." The true savior is the lamb that was slain for us who lives in Heaven. If you cannot take "it" to heaven, then it certainly cannot be the savior.

____

[24] IBID.
[25] IBID.

10 - Revelation Chapter 6

Chapter six is the beginning of the pronouncements when the lamb opens each of the seven seals. In this chapter, only six of the seven seals will be opened. It is not until chapter 8 that the seventh seal is opened. The four riders of the apocalypse are introduced in this chapter. They appear as the first four seals are opened. The opening of the first four seals fits a pattern. "Each one in turn prompts a summons from one of the creatures around the throne and is a prelude to action, as is the case with all the sequences of seven (except for Revelation 8:1, 11:19, 15:5)."[26]

The first four seals may have been inspired by Zechariah 1:8 and 6:1-3. The colors of the horses are different in the two descriptions. "In Zechariah, the horses patrol the earth (Zechariah 1:10) and are the four spirits of heaven (Zechariah 6:5)."It's not the same here. They proclaim future events.

The white horse is first. The rider wears a crown like that of the elders. The bow that he is carrying is the same word corresponding to the rainbow seen in Ezekiel's vision of heaven. The color white is associated with God or Christ. Therefore, one interpretation of this rider is that he symbolizes the Gospel, the proclamation of salvation. The first horseman goes out to conquer the Earth. There is no description of destruction associated with this horseman. [27]

Another interpretation for the white horseman comes from the imagination of the first-century reader. The dreaded Parthians were the only mounted archers in the first century, and the white horse was their trademark. Parthia was on the eastern border of the Roman Empire. The Romans never subdued this nation. "The defeat of the Roman armies in the Tigris valley

---

[26]Keck L., ed., "John Sees the Seals Opened," *The New Interpreters Bible Commentary*, vol. 12, *Hebrews, James, Peter, John, Jude, Revelation*, Keck, L., 608-617 (Nashville, TN: *Abingdon, 1998*;).
[27] IBID.

by the Parthian general Vologeses in 62 CE. was still remembered in John's time."[28] So for the listener or reader of John's time, this white horse was not Christ but the Parthians.

The second rider is given a sword with which he breaks the internal bonds that were holding the government together. Anarchy fills the earth. The third rider is on top of a black horse. He is holding a pair of scales. Food rationing, famine, and other problems will fall.

Nevertheless, the wealthy are not affected. Only the poor will pay the price of rising prices. The fourth rider is named "death." Death surrounds the book of Revelation and is a feature found throughout the judgment section.[29]

The scene changes as the fifth seal is opened. John sees those who have been slain because of the Word of God. These are people who decided to follow the Word of God and were killed because of it. Obedience to the Word of God is a key to salvation. They are given a white robe telling them that they will be in heaven. However, they must wait a bit longer until judgment day.

The sixth seal brings the beginning of the destruction of the world. The sun turned black like sackcloth. An earthquake occurs, probably signifying the power of God. The earthquake as a final day's event can be found in Jeremiah 10:22 (Septuagint version); Ezekiel 38:19 and Joel 2:10. The darkening of the sun can be found in Isaiah 50:3 and the moon in Ezekiel 32:7. The star falling from the sky is in Isaiah 13:10, and heaven is being rolled up in Isaiah 34:4 and Hebrews 1:12.[30]

---

[28] Boring M., *Interpreters - A Bible Commentary for Teaching and Preaching*, *Revelation* vols. (Louisville, KT: Knox Press
, 1989). Page 122
[29] Keck, "John Sees the Seals Opened".
[30] IBID.

The falling stars could be a reminder about the letters from chapters two and three, where the churches were described as stars. The destruction of the churches would be like the stars falling from heaven. Each time a church closes because of apathy and lack of evangelism, a star falls out of God's sky.

Summary of the Six Seals

1 – (6:1-2) the first horseman conquers.

2 – (6:3) the second horseman removes peace from the earth, so humans would slay one another.

3 – (6:5-6) the third horseman creates famine and inflated prices for food.

4 – (6:7-8) the fourth horseman with the sword causes ¼ of the people on the earth to be killed by the sword, famine, death, and wild beasts.

5 – (6:9) the martyrs plead for vindication

6 – (6:12-17) – earthquakes; sun-darkened; stars fall from heaven; heaven rolls up; kings and mighty hide themselves from God's presence.

The seventh seal is opened in chapter 8.

11 - Revelation 7

Chapter 7 of Revelation starts with a pause in the destruction. The angels standing at the four corners of the earth are instructed to hold the four winds to prevent any destruction from coming to the earth. This enables another angel from the east to place a seal on the forehead of the servants of God. [31]

The servants of God are 144,000 people who come from the Tribes of Israel. When the list of tribes is compared with a list of Jacob's sons found in Genesis 35:22; 49, Dan is absent from the list, while Manasseh is on the list. Manasseh is one of Joseph's sons. Joseph's other son, Ephraim, is missing from the list. Joseph is listed here, but is not listed as a tribe of Israel when the inheritance of the land was distributed. Also, this list in Revelation starts with Judah and not with Reuben (Reuben was Jacob's first-born son). The Messiah came from the tribe of Judah, so perhaps John listed the tribes in this order. What is also of interest is that the Assyrian army destroyed the ten tribes that composed the Northern Kingdom. How can these people be sealed by God when they do not exist in John's time? Only the tribes of Judah and Benjamin existed during John's writing. These two tribes had intermarried so often that it was next to impossible to separate the clans. Perhaps this list refers to people who lived in the past. If that is true, they would not be living through the end times. This theme of delaying for the sealing of the people is an echo of Ezekiel 9:4-5.[32] A Hebrew Scriptures echo about sealing can be found in Daniel 12:4.

Besides the 144,000, there is a great multitude that John describes. There is no mention of this group being sealed, and thus they will not receive the protection that the 144,000 will receive. Since they are wearing white robes and worshiping the Lamb, they must be a part of those who will be saved from the torture that is about to fall. The song they sing is a reminder of

---

[31] Leander Keck, ed., *Concerning Those Sealed and a Vision of the Great Multitude*, The New Interpreters Bible Commentary - Volume XII vols. (Nashville, TN: Abingdon Press, 1998).
[32] IBID.

the "Hosanna" song sung when Jesus entered Jerusalem. This song is also echoed in Psalm 118:21, 25.

John is met by an elder who asks him about the multitude of people in the white robes. How would John know who these people are? So, he turns the question back. The elder tells him that these people will come out of the great tribulation washed in the lamb's blood and made white. So, there is hope for those who truly worship God. The hope is that the righteous in God will be cleansed by the blood of the lamb and brought into God's sense. However, they do not have the seal of the Lamb upon their foreheads.

An exciting avenue to pursue is why the children of Israel have the seal of God upon them while the multitudes that follow Israel do not? Of course, being clothed in white after being washed in the lamb's blood is a sign of righteousness. Are there two different signs being given to us by God? Why would Israel be allowed into the presence of the lamb if they have not accepted the lamb as God's Messiah? Why are not the others sealed like Israel?

12 - Revelation 8 & 9

The seventh seal is opened at the beginning of chapter 8. For a moment, there is silence in heaven, as echoed in Habakkuk 2:20; Zephaniah 1:7; and Zechariah 2:13. The pause reminds us of the psalmist's words, "Be still, and know that I am God!" from Psalm 46:10. Silence is a characteristic of the eschatological age found in 4 Ezra 7:30-31. Ezra says that the world will be turned back to primeval silence for seven days.[33]

John now sees seven angels standing before the throne of God. Each of the angels is given a trumpet. In Joel 2:1, the trumpet blasts signaled an alarm that the world was coming into God's remarkable presence (also refer to Exodus 19:16). The trumpet blasts will now spell doom for the people of the earth.

The first trumpet brings hail mingled with blood (an echo of Exodus 9:23; Ezekiel 38:22; Sirach 39:29). One-third of the earth is destroyed. The second trumpet causes a fiery mountain to be cast into the sea. In 79 CE, Mount Vesuvius erupted, and this picture may have been in John's mind when he described the second blast. The third trumpet brings a fiery "bolt" from heaven, a star from heaven. The rivers and springs of the earth are the targets. John names the star "Wormwood," used in Amos 5:6-7; 6:12, where justice is turned to wormwood (also refer to Jeremiah 9:15).[34]

The fourth trumpet blast strikes the sun. An eagle cries out a woe to the earth's inhabitants because of what will happen during the subsequent three trumpet blows. The fifth trumpet blast starts a star falling from heaven. A bottomless pit (an abyss) is created. The smoke that rises from the abyss is not a smoke pleasing unto God but a smoke like that from a furnace that darkens the sun and pollutes the air. Locusts appear out of the smoke and torment those

---

[33] Leander Keck, ed., *The Seventh Seal and the Seven Angels with Seven Trumpets*, The New Interpreters Bible Commentary - Volume XII vols. (Nashville, TN: Abingdon Press, 1998).
[34] IBID.

whom God does not seal. We do not know if the multitudes in the white robes are saved from the torment that the locusts will cause.

The locusts are warhorses prepared for a battle. "The comparison of their teeth with that of a lion echoes Joel 1:6, and the sound of their wings is loosely echoed in Joel 2:5."[35] The locust king is named Abaddon, another name for Sheol (the grave, the realm of the dead). John ensures that his Greek readers know this king by using the Greek word Apollyon, which means the "destroyer" from the underworld.

The sixth trumpet is followed by a voice coming from the golden altar that is before God. The four angels that are at the river Euphrates are to release the river. Another third of humankind is killed. John then hears horsemen, two hundred million. John speaks of a general similarity between these creatures and Job's leviathan (Job 41:10), similar teeth, breastplate, smoke, and fire.

Revelation then discusses how the people of the earth who have not been killed continue in their pagan worship and refuse to repent of their sins.

____

[35] IBID.

13 – Revelation 10 and 11

Chapter 10 of the book of Revelation continues with the descent of an angel from heaven. This angel is dressed in a cloud with a rainbow over his head. This is a description of Christ's return found in Matthew 13:26 and 1 Thessalonians 4:17). There is a connection between chapter 10 and Ezekiel 2:10 and 3:3. John is commanded to write what the seven thunders have said from heaven and seal the scroll. The visualization of open and sealed scrolls continues. Most likely, what John was commanded to write could not be good for the peoples of the earth. The angel's great shout is equivalent to a lion's roar echoed from Amos 3:8. "It prompts a response from the seven thunders."[36]

The words from Daniel 12:7 is used here to describe an oath by the God of earth and heaven. John references God as Creator based on Exodus 20:1 (also refer to Ps 146:6, Acts 4:24). The mystery of God will be fulfilled when the seventh trumpet is blown.

John is commanded to take the scroll from the angel in the fashion of Ezekiel, echoed in Ezekiel 2:8. John then ate the scroll and is therefore commissioned to prophesy to the nations. The sweetness of the scroll, which then turns the stomach, is an echo found in Jeremiah 15:10. The prophecy that John will bring to the people will not be pleasant.

We can look at this chapter of the Revelation as the commissioning of John. From this point on, John is a prophet of God of the same caliber as Jeremiah, Isaiah and Ezekiel.

At the beginning of chapter eleven, John is given a measuring rod and told to measure the Temple of God and the altar. The outer court is excluded because that is the area that gentiles were allowed in. In Ezekiel 43:10-11, the temple measurement appears like a blueprint for the

---

[36] Leander Keck and, the Vision of the Strong Angel and the Command to Prophesy, *The New Interpreter's Bible Volume XII*, Nashville, TN vols. (Abingdon Press: 1998).

rebuilding of Jerusalem.[37] However, the Temple at Jerusalem had been destroyed. How can John measure it? Was he taking measurements of a Temple in heaven? Why is this important? What this does is to show to us that John was more than just a spectator. He was directly involved in the vision.

John is told that two witnesses will prophesy for 1,260 days (just under two and one-half years). They will wear sack clothes. Sackcloth was worn during times of mourning. After two and one-half years, they will be killed by the beast of the Abyss. The beast is not described to us, and the death of the two witnesses is also a mystery. The bodies of these witnesses will lie in the street of the great city (either Sodom or Egypt is conjectured). Being refused burial was a sign of the ultimate indignity. This tells us that the birds and animals that roamed the streets could tear these bodies apart. This opposes all Jewish burial laws.

An earthquake follows, with 7,000 people dying. The people acknowledge it is God who is causing these things to happen. Will they follow God entirely after these disasters?

The day of judgment has come to the earth, the day when heaven and earth come together. The twenty-four elders in the throne room of God give thanks for this event. The dead are then judged.

Heaven opens, and the Ark of the Covenant can be seen. There are flashes of lightning and thunder that always accompany God.

---

[37] Leander Keck, *The Two Witnesses*, The New Interpreter's Bible Volume XII vols. (Nashville, TN: Abingdon Press, 1998).

14 - Revelation Chapter 12

There are two visions that John recorded in this chapter. The first vision is that of a woman pursued by a dragon and the holy war between the hosts of angels led by Michael and Satan.

A pregnant woman appears "clothed with the sun" (Revelation 12:1) with the moon under her feet. She is also wearing a crown with twelve stars on her head. The woman is crying out from labor pains. In the Christian Scriptures, the reference to labor pain is used as a metaphor for the birth of the reign of God (Matthew 24:8; Mark 13:8; 1 Thessalonians 5:3).[38] In 1 Thessalonians 5:3, the labor pains are a metaphor for the second coming of the Lord at the end of time.

Another sign in heaven appears next to the pregnant woman. This sign is a great dragon whose identity is described in verse 9. The actual effects of the dragon will be disclosed in chapter 13. The dragon's appearance echoes the beast described in Daniel 8:10. The dragon intends to devour the child that is about to be borne by the woman.[39] The woman flees into the desert while the child is snatched from the earth by God. "As the gospels indicate, the desert is the place where the voice cries out, and the Messiah emerges, on the very margins of life (Matthew 3:3)."[40]

The woman's flight is reminiscent of that of the parents of Jesus when they fled to Egypt. Another echo for the woman is when Hagar fled from Sarah (Genesis 16:7 & Genesis 21:14). She remains in the desert for 1260 days, which is the same time that two witnesses from chapter 11 prophesied.

---

[38] Leander Keck, ed., *Signs in Heaven: The Woman and the Dragon*, The New Interpreter's Bible Commentary Volume XII vols. (Nashville, TN: Abingdon Press, 1998).
[39] IBID.
[40] IBID.

Some scholars have equated this vision to Mary, Jesus' mother. Eventually, God will snatch Jesus back into heaven. However, the vision is clear that the child is snatched right after its birth. A way of interpreting this vision is that the woman trusted God because God would ensure that the dragon would not get her baby. God keeps His promises and delivers the child safely from his mother's womb. In addition, God saved the mother from the dragon.

With verse 7 we enter a heavenly war. It is through this war that Satan was ejected out of heaven again. The dragon is Satan, who tries to regain control of heaven. It is not God who defends heaven but his creatures, the angels. The problem with this section is that during the time between Jesus' death and his resurrection, he was fighting Satan for the final battle. Now, in Revelation 12, we find a different theology. The final battle occurs at the end of time. It would fit the theology that Satan is still working in the world and now in heaven to regain control of God. At the end of time, Satan is finally defeated.

The chapter continues with a victory party of sorts. The woman is given a pair of wings. Unfortunately, the enraged dragon went off to make war against all who obeyed Jesus Christ.

15 - Revelation 13

Chapter 12 concluded with the dragon standing on the seashore, furious and ready to wage war against the offspring of the pregnant woman. Two additional beasts are described in chapter 13. The consequences suffered by the inhabitants of the Earth because of Satan's expulsion from Heaven are described in this chapter. John sees the inhabitants of the Earth falling in line with the beast and worshiping it.

The new beast that comes out of the sea has ten horns and seven heads with ten crowns on his horns. Each crown had a blasphemous name engraved in it. The beast resembles a leopard but has feet like a bear and the mouth of a lion. "Three of Daniel's beasts are merged into one (refer to Daniel 7:4-6). The dragon from chapter 12 gives all its power to this beast. Is Satan giving his power to the beast? The text reads that way.

Earth's inhabitants worship this beast. Only God deserves our worship, so this beast is helping the people of the Earth to sin before God. The beast is given forty-two months to exercise his authority on Earth. This is an echo found in Ezekiel 20:26.[41] The beast speaks as the fourth beast in the book of Daniel (Daniel 7:8, 11, 20). The beast curses Heaven and the Saints in heaven (as in the beast's horn in Daniel 7:21).

All the people worship this beast except those whose names are written in the Book of Life and belong to the Lamb that was slain (Jesus). The names in the book will not be revealed until judgment occurs (refer to Daniel 12:1). The Lamb slain before the foundation of the world refers to a pre-existent truth that reflects the world of apocalyptic mysteries and truths,

---

[41] Leander Keck, ed., *The Two Beasts*, New Interpreters Bible Commentary Volume XII vols. (Nashville, TN: Abingdon Press, 1998).

where things are known from eternity even if they are only revealed eschatologically (refer to Romans 16:20; Ephesians 3:9; and Colossians 1:26).[42]

The vision is interrupted by two aphorisms which echoes in Jeremiah 15:2 and 43:11. The first speaks of the acceptance of captivity if one becomes captive (verse 10). "The second promises death by the sword for those who resist with the sword." [43] The aphorisms cause a break in the narrative about the first beast and the second beast.

This second beast comes from the land. This second beast causes all the peoples of the earth to worship the first beast. The sign of fire in verse 13 echoed the sign of Elijah in 1 Kings 18:38 when he was battling the priests of Baal.[44] The first beast had a mortal wound that was healed. The second beast was attempting to force the people to worship this first beast. "The beast whose mortal wound was healed may reflect Nero, who was assassinated in 68 CE, but was widely rumored to have escaped death and fled to the east, whence he was on the point of coming back as emperor. This legend is included in the "Suetonious' Life of Nero."[45]

The mysterious number 666 has fascinated scholars for many years. In the ancient world, letters were used to represent numbers. The numerical value of the name Nero Caesar when transliterated from Greek to Hebrew is 666.

The 'Sibylline Oracles' indicates that 666 represents a contrast with the numerical value of Jesus in Greek, which is 888, a contrast that fits in well with the parody of Christ and the image of the beast in the next chapter.[46] Could the use of the mark of the beast contrast with God's mark of the 144,000? Perhaps, Satan is marking the souls who still lived on the Earth for

---

[42] IBID.
[43] IBID.
[44] Keck, *The Two Beasts*.
[45] IBID.
[46] IBID.

himself. Those who have the number 666 on their foreheads will be traveling with Satan when the time is right.

16 - Revelation Chapter 14

John sees another vision of justice as a terrible harvest. John first sees the Lamb standing on Mount Zion with the 144,000 who have the name and mark of God on their foreheads. The picture of Mount Zion as a site of salvation is echoed in Isaiah 2, Micah 4, and the crucifixion of Jesus. The only mention of God as the Father of the Lamb in the book of the Revelation is here. In another place, God is referred to as the Father of the Son of Man. The 144,000 have, besides the mark of God, the name of God written on their foreheads. The name of God is sacred. God's name was only spoken in the Holy of Holies in the Temple at Jerusalem and only on the Day of Atonement.[47] The 144,000 sing a new song from heaven, as did the elders and creatures around the throne, to mark the Lamb's taking of the scroll (refer to Revelation 5:8 and Ps 144:9).

Virginity and defilement (or rather non-defilement) are linked here and imply abstinence from sexual activity. In Leviticus 15:18, the Law says that sexual activity can cause uncleanness, which requires ritual cleansing to avoid defiling the tabernacle (Leviticus 15:31) and the holy mountain (Exodus 19:15). Purity and a sense of distinctiveness is idiomatically connected to sexual relations.[48]

Rapture of the living occurs. Those who have been assumed into heaven at this point are called the "first fruits," which implies that the total of the elect has not been taken into heaven (note that Christ has not returned yet).

The message from the angel in verse 7 is simple: "Fear God and give Him glory, for the hour of his judgment has come." In Joshua 7:19, giving glory to God is closely linked to the

---

[47] Leander Keck and Ed., the Lamb, The 144,000, the Eternal Gospel, and the Human Figure, *The New Interpreters Bible Commentary Volume X11*, Nashville, TN vols. (Abingdon Press: 1998).
[48] IBID.

confession of sin. Judgment day for the living has arrived. Those who have been worshiping the beast will discover that only God is to be worshiped.

The second angel speaks about the fall of Babylon. "Babylon's offense was having caused all the nations to 'drink the wind of the wrath of her fornication' (Jeremiah 15:7)."[49] This statement can be interpreted as Babylon had intoxicated the people and caused wrath because of the forgetfulness of the true vocation to worship (Babylon led the people of Israel away from Yahweh worship by destroying the Temple and trying to impose their pagan religion on them). The same thing is happening with the beast whom the people are worshiping instead of God.

The third angel announces the torment of those who worship the beast. The wine of God's fury is an image of God's anger as strong as undiluted wine (refer to Isaiah 51:17 and Jeremiah 25:15). God's fury comprises fire, as seen by burning sulfur, which is found with burning brimstone. The saints are told to endure, which comprises keeping God's commandments and holding fast to faith in Jesus. It is their endurance that will prevent them from worshiping the beast.[50]

Those who die in the Lord from now on will rest from their deeds. Dying in the Lord is a prerequisite to enter heaven, which requires repenting of all evil deeds (refer to Revelation 9:20 and Revelation14:14-20).

Verses 14-20 is a harvest reaping metaphor. The good grapes are harvested by the "son of man," while the bad grapes are harvested by another angel who tosses his grapes into the great winepress of God's wrath.

---

[49] IBID.
[50] IBID.

Of great debate is where is the "rapture" in Revelation? Following Paul's analysis, the rapture does not occur until the Son of Man returns. Following the vision of Revelation, the rapture begins here in chapter 14. It is found in two different places in chapter 14. If we read ahead, we discover that more of the faithful are brought into heaven. Are these faithful "leftovers" from the first two raptures, or do the wicked change their views and become worshipers of God and not the beast?

What are the modern-day beasts that we worship instead of God? How can people be brought to see that they must worship God and not the beast?

17 - Revelation 15

John has another vision in heaven. We are introduced to seven angels who hold the last of the seven plagues that God will unleash upon the Earth. The end of the world's torture is about to arrive; the wrath of God will end.

The sea of glass was introduced to us in Revelation 4:6 (also found in a description of heaven in 1 Enoch 14). The sea is mixed with fire (like the hail mixed with fire seen earlier). John sees those who have conquered the beast, its image, and the number of its name. Those who defeated the beast remind us of the great multitude of Revelation 7:9 and the 144,000 in Revelation 14:1. This multitude sings praises to God as they are holding "harps of God." They are singing the "song of Moses" found in Exodus. This was the song the people sang after they had crossed the Red Sea (Exodus 15:1-18). The analogy here is that those who have conquered the temptations of the beast and remained faithful to God will be found on the side of the sea of glass, which places them in the Temple of God in Heaven.[51]

The "temple of the tent of witness" is opened (verse 5), rather than an Ark of the covenant, and seven angels appear. The angels are clothed in clean, shining linen. Their garb is possibly inspired by the stories of judgment on Jerusalem in Ezekiel 9:3-4. One of the four creatures in the throne room gives a golden bowl to each of the angels. Perhaps the question asked by the souls under the altar will be answered; "how long?" The Temple fills with smoke, which represents God's glory (an echo from Exodus 40:34). No one can enter the Temple until the plague has been unleashed (an echo of Ex. 40:35 and 1 Kings 8:10-11).

---

[51] Leander Keck, *Another Sign in Heaven*, The New Interpreter's Bible Commentary - Volume XII vols. (Nashville, TN: Abingdon Press, 1998).

The Sea of Glass with the people on one side waiting to go through the Sea to God echoes Exodus. The people remained at the shore as the Egyptian chariots approached, and when they received salvation by God opening the Red Sea, allowing them to pass through without harm (or even getting wet). What is important to note is that the people sing praises to God and the Lamb before they get across the sea. In Exodus, the song of Moses is sung after Israel successfully crosses the Sea. A different level and maturity of faith, perhaps?

In chapter 15, a connection can be made between Caesar and Pharaoh. The eschatological woes are the plagues that hit Egypt. Egypt is symbolic of Rome (Rome being a "modern" day Egypt). The song in verse 15 pronounces the glory of the victorious God to whom all nations come to worship. In times of trouble, we need to praise and thank God (an apocalyptic theme) continually.

A side note is that the Greek word for "bowl" connotes a bowl used in offerings at the Temple and synagogue. A first-century Greek listener or reader would recognize the "bowl" as the word used in the Septuagint.[52] Is John telling us something about our offerings to God? If the offerings are not a biblical tithe, could the bowls use to collect God's be used against us?

---

[52] M. Boring, *Interpreters - A Bible Commentary for Teaching and Preaching*, *Revelation* vols. (Louisville, KT: Knox Press
, 1989).

Revelation 16

In chapter 16, we have the pouring out of the bowls of God's wrath upon the people of the Earth. In the same manner, as has been seen before, there is a pause between the sixth and seventh bowl, where a more extended description is offered about what is happening. This chapter focuses upon God's Day of Judgment to the living.[53] The location for judgment is in front of the Temple, where John hears a loud voice that proclaims the start of the pouring out of the bowls. The loud voice of the proclamation of God is found in Rev. 1:10; 11:12; 12:10; 14:13; 16:17; 21:3 and in Isaiah 66:6.[54]

The first angel pours out his bowl and sores afflict humankind. This is an echo found in Exodus 9:10-11. God poured out plagues on the Egyptians because they would not let God's people go. Humanity will blaspheme God and will not repent because of the sores, especially those with the beast's mark and who worship its image (this is an echo of Ezekiel 9:4).

The second angel pours out his wrath onto the sea, which turns into blood. This image echoed the story when Moses' staff touched the Nile River, turning it to blood (Exodus 7:17-18). The fish of the sea die because of this transformation.

God is then hailed for His judgments (this echo is in several of the minor prophets' books). A theme of the Revelation is "God as a judge." The angel's hymn in verses 5-7 is based on Lex talionis (Exodus 21:24). "As they deserve" in verse 6 is a loose translation but brings home the message that humankind is receiving what it deserves because of the evil that has been done. Drinking blood is prohibited by Leviticus 17:10. If the people are sinning against God, why would they obey Leviticus?

---

[53] Leander Keck, ed, *Revelation 16:1-21*, The New Interpreters Bible Volume XII vols. (Nashville, TN: Abingdon Press, 1998).
[54] IBID.

Matthew 13:6 speaks about the sun being permitted to scorch humanity. The cursing and the blasphemed name of God mentioned can be found in Isaiah 52:5. God implements the plague, and the people still refuse to repent of their sins.[55] The beast and his kingdom are plunged into darkness (referring to Satan), which echoes Exodus 10:22. "Revelation echoes the sentiments of the Fourth Gospel: 'People loved the darkness rather than light (John 3:19 NRSV)." [56]

The drying up of the Euphrates makes the way clear for the "kings from the east" to come, as echoed in Isaiah 11:15, and John says they are gathering for a battle. The day of the Lord described in verses 10-14 is an echo of Amos 5:18. There is then an interruption in the sequence of the seven bowls.

Armageddon and the Mount Megiddo are a place where the final battle of the Earth will occur. That is a general interpretation of verse 16. If we look at the details of what is written about Mount Megiddo, we can see that this place is not on a map. It is assumed that John is writing some prediction of a future event. Perhaps he is trying to describe something that he is hopeful for in his own time. The persecutions against the Christians were deepening. The best thing that could have occurred for the Christians was for Rome to be overthrown.

There is no battle described in chapter 16. Also, John could easily use military terms to describe his theology of the victory that Jesus had over the cross (refer to Revelation 5:1-14 and Revelation 12:7-12). "Revelation thus contains no descriptions of eschatological battles (refer to Revelation 19:11-21; 20:7-10)."[57] John indicates that he is giving us the Hebrew name of the place where the battle will occur. The first part of the word "har" in Hebrew means "mountain." John is saying that the battle will occur at the Mountain of Megiddo. "Since there

---

[55] IBID.

[56] IBID.

[57] M. Boring, *Interpreters - A Bible Commentary for Teaching and Preaching, Revelation* vols. (Louisville, KT: Knox Press, 1989). Page 177

is no such place in the Hebrew Scriptures or Israeli geography, the hearer-readers' mind is teased into activity – precisely what John's evocative language calls for." [58]

There is no mountain named Megiddo. The closest mountain is Mount Carmel. On this mountain, Elijah fought the prophets of Baal (1 Kings 18:20-46). For John, the Parthians were a force that could destroy the Empire. We met them when we were introduced to the four horsemen. The Parthians were the people from the east of the Euphrates who were archers who rode white horses. This was the only well-known organized group of people that the Romans could not defeat in 100 CE. In a world under Roman oppression, the thought of an enemy defeating the Empire would have been very pleasing. The mystery of what John is trying to tell us remains unless it is viewed as something for his time and not ours. At the end of time, there will be no battle at Mount Megiddo because this geographic point does not exist. The Parthians threatened the Empire after the assassination of Emperor Nero. The Empire went into a time of disarray and confusion. John recalls these battles hoping the Parthians would return and finish what they had started.

There is a large amount of destruction associated with the last bowl. Earthquakes, thunder, and lightning have been associated with destruction earlier in Revelation and are repeated.

When this chapter is examined, we can see that we could inflict upon ourselves these plagues in today's technological society. Nuclear weapons can easily cause what we are reading about. If a nuclear war were to occur, the destruction described in the Revelation would be the result. Perhaps Revelation is a warning from God to us today that now we have the power to destroy the Earth. Hopefully, our intelligence and common sense will catch up with our scientific capabilities. We will learn how not to destroy ourselves one day.

---

[58] IBID. Page 176

Revelation 17

Chapter 17 introduces Babylon, the woman. There is probably a connection between John's use of the name Babylon and the historical record of what Babylon did to Judah. Babylon destroyed the Temple in Jerusalem and attempted to get the priests and scribes of Israel to convert to pagan worship. In this chapter, an angel gives John some explanation of what will happen at the end of time.

At the beginning of the chapter, one of the seven angels offered to show John the punishment of Babylon, the great prostitute. Babylon, the great whore seated on the rivers, echoes Jeremiah 51:13, where he said that Babylon lives by the mighty waters. "Babylon, with whom the kings of the earth have committed formation (v. 2) resembles Tyre (see Isaiah 23:17 and Nahum 3:4), and her 'golden cup' has made all the earth drunk (Jeremiah 51:7)." [59] Babylon is also drunk with the blood of the witnesses of Jesus Christ. This would show that she has killed many of the saints of God.

The Spirit then takes John into the desert, an echo of Ezekiel 8:3. John comes face to face with Babylon in the desert in the same manner that Jesus came face to face with Satan in Matthew 4:1. The desert is a metaphor for insight and renewal, which is an echo of Hosea 2:14.[60] In the desert, John sees a woman with a beast full of blasphemous names, an echo of Daniel 7:25. The beast has seven heads and ten horns, like the beast that arose from the sea. The woman is clothed in purple and scarlet, not white, and adorned with gold, precious stones, and pearls. In Revelation 18:12, a list of clothes and stones that Babylon traded around the world is revealed. Therefore, she would be adorned in this manner. She is holding a golden cup 'full of abominations and impurities in her hand. "We have here the first of several ideas and images derived from Ezekiel's dramatic condemnation of Tyre starting in Ezekiel 28:13."[61]

---

[59] Leander Keck, *The Vision of Babylon*, The New Interpreters Bible Commentary Volume XII vols. (Nashville, TN: Abingdon Press, 1998).
[60] IBID.
[61] IBID.

Oddly, this woman resembles the saints in having a name rather than just a mark on her forehead. The woman's name is Babylon. During the following chapters, there is much discussion about the fall of Babylon, echoing Jeremiah 51. "Babylon's drunken stupor is infectious, and it contaminates those with whom she commits her fornications."[62] Fornication refers to anything that transgresses what constitutes appropriate relations (refer to Leviticus 18:6). The woman having a name, a divine image, reminds us of the beast with the healed fatal wound.

The angel decides to explain to John what this image means. The beast came out of the Abyss. The beast has the same literary combination attributed to it as was used for God: "once was, now is, and yet will come." Those whose names are not written in the book of life from the beginning of creation will be astonished about seeing the beast. This reference gives credence to those who believe that the book of Life was written before creation. Therefore, according to Revelation, God knew who would be coming to heaven before He created the heavens.

"True wisdom may consist, therefore, in making a correct identification of Babylon and the beast so that John and others like him are not deceived, as will be many of the inhabitants of the earth."[63] The seven heads stand for both seven mountains and seven kings. Five of the kings have fallen already, one is alive, and the final king has not come yet. In verse 11, the beast is said to be an eighth king who 'belongs to the seven' and will 'go to destruction.' The ten horns are the ten kings who are still to come. The kings share a common purpose, and that is to make war against the Lamb of God.[64]

The "many waters" upon which the woman Babylon is seated are the peoples of the nations. Verse 16 speaks about the kings coming together to destroy the prostitute Babylon. So, the

---

[62] IBID.
[63] IBID..
[64] IBID.

beast who once supported Babylon now will turn against her and devour her. This is an example of a kingdom divided against itself laid to waste (refer to Matthew 12:25).[65] If Rome is Babylon, then the seven heads may be references to Roman emperors. Since it is difficult to date Revelation precisely, it is hard to determine which seven emperors John refers to. Rome devoured all who stood in her way, even the nations which initially helped her to greatness. Eventually, Rome herself was consumed.

If we view this chapter as John's attempt to speak to the people of his time, he is handling his day's social and political realities. As echoed in the book of Daniel, it would not be prudent to write about the current oppressive government. That would undoubtedly lead to death. So, John's political agenda hides in imagery to keep the Roman authorities lost as to its true meaning. Rome was the current center of pagan worship.

Using the imagery of Babylon would have been very familiar to readers and listeners of the Hebrew Scriptures. This could also be a sign that possibly more Jews were reading the Revelation than Christians. The best audience that is for impact would have been Jewish-Christians. They would recognize the wrath of God as explained by the prophets, and they would have readily accepted the impact of Babylon as identical to them as what Rome was doing.

Also, there is a sense of justice in this chapter. The Christians were being persecuted. Eventually, the tyrant of Rome depicted as the woman named Babylon would be destroyed by the very people who propped her support. As with empires of the past, once the support eroded, the Empires fell. The Roman Empire would be no different except for a few more years until the actual fall occurred. Of course, by 317 CE, all persecutions against Christians stopped.

---

[65] IBID.

The apocalyptic theme of things is bad, and things will get worse. Then God will intervene can be seen in this chapter. It is bad because the whore Babylon is corrupting the people. That will continue until the support of Babylon gives way and wages war against her. A war within the Roman Empire was not a good thing for Christians. Anarchy could reign during those periods. There would be no way to stop the killings. Eventually, things will get better, and the whore will be brought to justice.

Revelation Chapter 18 to 19:10

John sees another angel descending from heaven whose authority is so great that the whole earth is illuminated, echoing Isaiah 6:4. This angel proclaims the fall of Babylon. Babylon is considered a haven for the sins of the world and the beasts and the dragon. It is difficult to separate the different "Babylons" that exist in Revelation. Babylon in chapter 17 was the name of the woman sitting on top of the beast from the Abyss. Now she is a nation, and the kings of the earth have drunk the wine of her fornication. Either way, Babylon offers the sin of the world. The wealth of the material world may come from Babylon, but only Christ can provide the true wealth of eternal life with God (refer to Rev 3:17-18). [66]

God's people are called out of Babylon. The same thing occurred when the Exile from Babylon was over. God called His people to come back to the Promised Land and to rebuild the Temple. This is also a metaphor that the people of God who did not share in the sin of Babylon must leave sin's midst so that they do not share in sin, an echo of Jeremiah 51:45. Perhaps they are being called out to avoid the plagues that will fall upon Babylon, an echo of Ezekiel 9:4-5. This imagery is an echo found in the book of Genesis. In chapters 18-19, the story of Sodom and Gomorrah tells us that the only righteous people, Lot and his family, were told to evacuate the city before the wrath of God fell upon her.[67]

Verses 6-8 appears to be a plea to give Babylon the sins that she has caused. This type of retribution is an echo of Isaiah 40:2, Jeremiah 16:18, and especially Psalm 137. The kings of the earth who mourn over Babylon in verse 9 are those who profited on earth by the sin of Babylon. The merchants of the world will also cry over Babylon for the same reason. They made a lot of money and lived luxuriously because of Babylon's sin. Now they will have to find some honest work. Babylon is stripped of her earthly wealth as a part of the punishment

---

[66] Leander Keck, *The Fall of Babylon*, New Interpreters Bible Commentary Volume XII vols. (Nashville, TN Abingdon Press: 1998).
[67] IBID.

that awaits her. This is a lesson for us. Those who adorn themselves with the material wealth of life by sinning will find that they will stand naked in front of God at the end of time. Earthly possessions cannot be brought into heaven.

The scene at the beginning of chapter 19 takes us back to the throne room of God. The elders and four living creatures are worshiping God, who is seated on the throne. We hear God speaking to us. After which, the multitudes praise God.

There is a time of rejoicing coming up because the marriage of the Lamb is about to happen. The bride has made herself ready to receive the bridegroom.

Note that John falls at the feet of the angel and is immediately rebuked (Revelation 19:10). Only God must be worshiped, and by John falling at the feet in front of the angel, he is imitating what the elders were doing before God, and he is told that this is wrong. Only God can be worshiped!

This passage is preparing us for the return of Christ, the Lamb of God. It is also a chapter that speaks to us about wealth and possessions. Babylon was greedy and tried to grab whatever she could in any manner she could. The chapter discusses the linens, pearls, gold, and silver that would be a part of wealth. If we allow wealth to dictate our worship or lack of worship to God, then we could end up in the same place as Babylon. It is not money that is a curse or an evil, but how we use our wealth that can cause the problem. Those in the church who use their God-given wealth only to promote themselves will find this passage difficult. Those who know that God gets the tithe and uses even more of their wealth for the glory of God will see that God promises to take care of those who give, even if their giving is small because their wealth is small, and that the reward may not be on Earth but rather in heaven at the end of time.

How about the wealth of the Church? The Banners? Brass Cross? Candle Sticks? Position of things? Are they Babylon for us?

Revelation 19:11-21

A venue change occurs with Revelation 19:11 in that John has returned to Earth so that he may witness the return of Christ. We are not explicitly told that John has returned to Earth, but this has happened when he says, "I saw heaven open." John sees the rider on a white horse coming down from heaven. The description of this rider tells us that this is Jesus Christ returning to Earth. John never calls the rider Christ or the Messiah. Instead, he gives us a description of the rider, which matches the descriptions of Christ that we have from the early chapters of Revelation. The vision of Christ in Revelation 1:14 has flaming eyes. The double-edged sword from the river's mouth is references Revelation 1:16 and 2:12. His is called "faith and truth," which are characteristics of Jesus found in Revelation 3:14. He also bears the name of the Word of God, a Christian Scripture reference to Christ. [68]

The calling of the birds for the great supper of God is echoed from Ezekiel 39:17

Ezekiel 39:17 [17] "Son of man, this is what the Sovereign LORD says: Call out to every kind of bird and all the wild animals: 'Assemble and come together from all around to the sacrifice I am preparing for you, the great sacrifice on the mountains of Israel. There you will eat flesh and drink blood.

This is opposite to the idea of the marriage feast that follows a wedding. When the Lamb comes to marry its bride, the church, there will not be a feast but judgment. This theme is in line with the Parousia beliefs that Paul wrote about. The war against evil is not over. Even though the world has been thoroughly cleansed of sin of every kind, as seen in chapter 18, the ability of evil to come into God's world will continue to plague us.

---

[68] M. Boring, *Interpreters - A Bible Commentary for Teaching and Preaching*, *Revelation* vols. (Louisville, KT: Knox Press, 1989). Pg. 195

The battle that comes between Christ and Satan will not be a war through the force of arms, but the power of the Word of God will fight this last fight. The power of God's Word will be shown to us.[69] Those who worshiped the beast or his image will be judged by the Word of God. Revelation reminds us that God will not continue to sit by and watch human injustice. Eventually, God will take matters into His own hands. The first thing that Christ does upon His return is to destroy Satan with the Word of God. He does not deal with the faithful first, but with the false prophets and Satan worshipers.

The book of Revelation is a manual on what not to do. The warnings are for us to stay far away from Satan as is possible. It is written from a completely opposite approach to the rest of the Bible. Instead of telling us what we must do to receive eternal life with God, it tells us everything we must restrain from to receive God's eternal life in heaven.

---

[69] Leander Keck, *Heaven Opens, and the Rider on the White Horse Appears*, The New Interpreters Bible Commentary Volume XII vols. (Nashville, TN: Abingdon Press, 1998).

Revelation 20:1-15

This section is broken into three sections.

Revelation 20:1-6

John sees another angel descending from heaven who has the key to the Abyss and holds a great chain in his hand. The key to the Abyss was given to the star that fell from heaven in Revelation 9:1.[70] The great chain in his hand tells us that this angel will lock someone into prison (refer to Mark 5:3, Acts 12:6-7; Ephesians 6:20), a standard method used in ancient Rome. The angel seizes the dragon, who is Satan, and locks him away for 1,000 years. Subsequently, the angel throws the keys into the Abyss, effectively imprisoning Satan.

What is interesting is that in 1,000 years, Satan must be released from this prison. Why does Satan have to be released? Referring to Psalm 90:4, this is only one day to God. This does not help us understand why Satan must be released, but it references God's timing and not ours.

This chapter of Revelation is the most controversial chapter of the entire book. There appears to be information in this chapter that contradicts that which is written elsewhere in the book. For example, we are told that some of the dead will be resurrected. He calls this the first resurrection. However, in Revelation 11:18, at a trumpet blast, we are told it is time for the dead to be judged. But judgment does not occur without resurrection. At the time of the resurrection of the dead, they are judged, and either allowed into heaven or sent to the Abyss of Satan. So, how can this resurrection in chapter twenty be the first resurrection? Then the text itself notes that a second resurrection will occur after 1,000 years.

---

[70] Leander Keck, Ed, *Millennium and Judgment*, The New Interpreter's Bible Commentary Volume XII vols. (Nashville, TN: Abingdon Press, 1998).

There is some speculation that John is referring to different people. The righteous come to life in Christ at this first resurrection and become Christ's priests. So, are the non-believers still dead? What about those who died before Christ?

The locking up of Satan into prison is a reversal of what Satan had done to humankind since the fall in the Garden of Eden. This act also reverses the hold that the beast and Babylon had on the inhabitants of the Earth. However, it will only last for 1,000 years.

The messianic reign of Revelation is defined. For 1,000 years, Christ will rule on the Earth. We are not told what is going to happen during this time. Will we have a world that is wholly voided of evil and sin? If Satan is locked up, then one would think so. What about human nature? Will the 1,000-year reign of Christ be so glorious that human nature will be suppressed for that time?

The reason for this "lock-up" and the messianic reign is a mystery today. Throughout Christian history, many theologians have tried to explain it but usually turn up short.

Revelation 20:7-10

Satan is released from his 1,000-year captivity. Why is Satan released? The cosmic battle between God and Satan does not occur in this chapter. Instead, fire descends from heaven and consumes the enemy forces. This fire was an echo of Elijah on Mount Carmel when he fought the priests of Baal. Satan is thrown to the same place as the beast in chapter 19.

Early commentators viewed this section as being added to the text by a different writer. Why is this duplicate story of Satan's defeat in the Revelation? Suppose the Earth was cleansed in chapters 18 and 19. The beast with Satan was forced into the dark place with Satan's followers (those with his mark and who worshiped the idols); therefore, then Satan is done. Why do we need a second story?

Revelation 20:11-15

Revelation 11:18 tells us at the sounding of the seventh trumpet, it is time to judge the dead. In Revelation 20:12, John tells us he sees the dead and is now time for their judgment. He speaks about the Book of Life, and those whose name is written in the book will go on to Heaven, and those whose name is not will be tossed into the fire with Satan and the beast.

How can we ignore Revelation 11:18 that the dead have been judged? The verse says that it is time for judgment. That implies that judgment will occur. Again, we see a repeat of what has happened earlier in the book. The Christian tradition is that judgment will not occur until the return of Christ. In chapter 11, Christ had not yet returned. How can the judgment of the dead occur then? Based on John's vision, his theology differs from Paul's and the Gospel writings. Did a later author add in another judgment to make the Revelation more palatable to readers who were being taught a different theological position than Revelation was presenting?

It would seem so. For those who do not want to go in that direction, the standard line is that judgment did not occur in Revelation 11. Perhaps God changed His mind and postpone judgment of the dead until after Christ's return. Does God change His mind concerning His timetables? We do see God changing His mind when Abraham pleaded for the cities of Sodom and Gomorrah. If God changed his mind, then why could not he change it now?

Through this and other points in this chapter, it can be seen why we are engaging with a very controversial piece of scripture.

Revelation Chapter 21 – 22:5

The focus of Revelation is now about the new Earth as the new heavenly city descends. In this chapter, the dimensions of the new Jerusalem are revealed. When this vision was written, it should be noted that Jerusalem did not exist (it was destroyed in 70 CE by the Romans after the Second Jewish Revolt).

Since this chapter is full of images from the Hebrew Scriptures and earlier parts of Revelation, the following was developed.

21:1 – the new Heaven and Earth are found in Isaiah 65:17 and 66:22. "No more sea" – the sea in heaven in Revelation 4:6 became a threatening place to be endured or conquered (refer to Revelation 15:2), and the earthly sea was an object of judgment (refer to Rev 5:13; 7:1-2; 8:8-9; 12:12; 16:3; 18:21). The beast that rose to threaten the eternal destiny of humanity came from the sea (refer to Revelation 13:1). The threat of the sea is removed.

22:2 – that which descends from heaven is a blessing rather than a curse (refer to Rev 12:12; 16:21).

22:3 – God's tabernacle is found in heaven in Revelation 15:5, the source of the seven last plagues. It is the object of the beast's blasphemy in Revelation 13:6. This verse resonates with the theme that those redeemed come from "every tribe and language and people and nation," echoing Revelation 5:9 and 7:9.

21:4 – the promise of Revelation 7:17 is once again stated (refer to Isaiah 25:8), and the end of death is repeated (refer to Revelation 20:10). There will be no more mourning, crying, or pain (refer to Isaiah 35:10; 51:11; 65:19).

21:5-6 – John is directed to write things down in Revelation 1:11, 1:19; 14:13; 19:9. God is the alpha and omega (refer to Revelation 1:8), the beginning and the end. Alpha and omega are the first and last letters of the Greek alphabet. The giving of water as a gift is the promise of Revelation 7:6. The spring of water will be described in Revelation 22:1 (refer to Zechariah 14:8 and John 7:37). Water will no longer pose a threat (refer to Revelation 12:15; 15:2).

21:7 – The ones who have overcome the beast and its image by the blood of the Lamb will inherit "these things" (refer to Revelation 15:2; 21:11). The Davidic covenant from 2 Samuel 7:14 is extended to all people in the Jubilees 1:24. It is central to the eschatology of parts of the New Testament, especially Revelation.

21:8 – The promise made in verse 7 is followed by a darker statement in eschatological passages in the Christian Scriptures (refer to 1 Corinthians 6:10 and Galatians 5:21). The list of those condemned for the second death parallels Ezekiel 44:9, Romans 1:29, 1 Corinthians 6:10, and Titus 1:16.

21:9-11 – John is carried away "in the spirit," which is an echo of Revelation 4:1, and Ezekiel, who in visions was brought to a very high mountain to behold a city (refer to Ezekiel 40:1). John is taken to a high mountain (refer to Matthew 4:8; 17:1). John is shown the Holy City, which is different from Ezekiel's city.

21:12-14 – John describes the city in terms that evoke the conclusion of Ezekiel's vision of Jerusalem (refer to Ezekiel 48:30). The four gates at each compass point echo them in Ezekiel 48:31. Here, too, they are linked to the twelve tribes of Israel. Angels at the gates is an echo of Isaiah 62:6. Also, the names of the "twelve apostles of the Lamb" are inscribed on the walls. This is an echo of Ephesians 2:20, where the household of God is built on the foundation of the apostles and the prophets. This passage is the only one in the book of Revelation that refers to the apostles of the Lamb.

21:15 – The measuring of the city is in contrast with that described in Revelation 11:1 and Ezekiel 40:3. We do not know why measurement is being taken of the city.

21:16-17 – the city is "foursquare," a cube equal in height, width, and length. The interior of the inner sanctuary of Solomon's Temple was also a cube (refer to 1 Kings 6:20).

21:18-20 – The walls of the city are made of jasper. The city is built of pure gold, which is as "clear as glass." The jewels described are from the high priest's breastplate (refer to Exodus 28:17-20).

21:21 – the twelve gates are made of a single pearl which is transparent as glass (refer to 2 Corinthians 4:4; Hebrews 1:3; 2 Peter 1:19)

21:22-23 – John reports that the new city does not have a new Temple in it. The city is a sanctuary unto itself, since God will live in the city. There is no need for light in this city because the sin of Babylon is gone and all that remains is the brilliance of God. The description of God's glory echoes Ezekiel's vision (Ezekiel 1:28; 15:8; 18:1; 21:11).

21:24-27 – The promise that the nations will be ruled by the messianic rod has often appeared in Revelation (refer to Rev 12:5; 19:15). In Isaiah 60:11, the kings will lead their nations in a procession to bring their wealth into Zion, whose gates are never closed (refer to Zechariah 14:7). Only people whose names are written in the Book of Life may enter.

22:1 – John sees the river of the water of life, promised in Revelation 21:6. With its life-giving qualities, this river contrasts with the rivers that were poisoned in the eschatological catastrophes (refer to Revelation 8:10; 16:4; 16:12). It evokes paradise, a Garden (refer to Genesis 2:10).

22:2-5 – The tree in Ezekiel 47:12 produced twelve different fruit each month. The leaves of the tree are meant for the healing of the nations. Here the throne of God and the lamb is in the city. Heaven is now on earth, and God's servants will perform their service to God without a temple.

Revelation 22:6-21

This section of the Revelation is closing comments and a command to John about what he is to do with this vision. Also, there is a warning to us not to change it. Many people read those verses, believing that this warning pertains to the entire Bible. It only pertains to Revelation.

The vision that John has been having come to an abrupt stop in Revelation 22:5. Some isolated comments and saying are not tied to each other in these final verses. When compared to the first chapter of the book, there is the same pattern of isolation of thoughts. There is the mystery of who is speaking in verses 10 and 12 when the book's central theme is repeated.

Verse 6 begins with the angel speaking to John. Which angel is this? Is it an angel who held a plate of plagues, or is it the Son of Man? John identifies himself in verse 8 as the person who received this vision from God.

In verse 10, John is told not to lock up the prophecy that he has been given. In Daniel 12:9, Daniel is said to lock up and hide the prophecy of the End Time. Of all the books of the Bible, Revelation is the one most intended to lead the reader to change. A watchword of Revelation is "repent."

"Blessed are those whose robes are washed in the blood of the Lamb," reminding us that the righteous will not follow the beast no matter how hard the beast tries to pull us away from God.

In verse 16, the speaker identifies himself as Christ and says that He was the one who sent His angel to bear witness to the things that John saw. The Davidic covenant is again asserted to remind the readers that the offspring of David would sit on the throne.

In verse 17, we learn again that hearing of the Word of God must be accompanied by heeding the commands of God and not worshiping the beast. The authority of the prophecy is found in this book in verse 18.

"Amen. Come, Lord Jesus!" echoes the response found in earlier Christian liturgies like the Didache and the Maranatha[i].

John concludes the book with a prayer. Amen.

---

[i] Maranthaa is a Greek expression from two Aramaic words that appears in 1 Corinthians 16:22. It can mean "the Lord is coming!," "the Lord has come," "Our Lord comes." Source: https://www.maranatha.com/